EXPERIENCING
THE SPIRIT
SECOND EDITION

A STUDY ON THE WORK OF THE HOLY SPIRIT IN THE LIFE OF THE BELIEVER

DENZIL R. MILLER

All Scripture quotations, unless otherwise indicated, are taken from the NEW INTERNATIONAL VERSION ®, Copyright © 1960, 1962, 1963, 1968, 1972, 1973, 1975, 1977, 1995 by The Lockman Foundation. All rights reserved.

Library of Congress Cataloging-in-Publication Data
Miller, Denzil R., 1946–
Experiencing the Spirit: A Study on the Work of the Holy Spirit in the Life of the Believer
Denzil R. Miller

ISBN 978-0-9911332-4-6

1. Pneumatology—Pentecostal. 2. Biblical teaching— 3. Biblical studies—Holy Spirit

Printed in the United States of America
PneumaLife Publications
Springfield, MO, USA

– Contents –

– Introduction –

A mother was watching a column of soldiers marching through the city. As the column moved by, she saw her son, David, marching proudly with the rest. As he smiled and waved, everyone could see that he was out of step with the other soldiers. When everyone else's right foot went forward, David's went backward. When theirs went backward, his went forward. "Would you look at that?" the mother exclaimed, "Everyone is out of step except my David!"

The story of David is a parable of many Christians today. They are out of step, not only with other Christians, but with the Spirit of God. Paul admonished believers, "Keep in step with the Spirit" (Gal. 5:25). In this study we will discuss how a believer in Christ may live a life in step with the Spirit of God—one that is lived under the Spirit's direction and control. It is my sincere desire that, as a result of this study, you will experience the Spirit in your life in a new and powerful way, and that you will enter into a new and deeper relationship with Him.

This study is meant to be more than just an intellectual exercise. It has been designed as a practical guide for a spiritually dynamic life. To receive maximum benefit, it is essential that the teacher and student, once they have encountered a new truth, immediately apply that truth to their own spiritual lives. It will do little good, for example, if one learns about the baptism in the Holy Spirit and yet fails to be personally baptized in the Spirit. Life in the Spirit is not a thing to be read about. It is rather a life to be experienced and lived daily.

These lessons are based on the author's book, *In Step with the Spirit: Studies in the Spirit-filled Walk.* That book deals with each of the subjects (as well as other subjects) contained in this study, yet in a more comprehensive manner. The book can be obtained by contacting the PneumaLife Publications.

Denzil R. Miller, D.Min.
Galatians 2:20

Meet Your Remarkable Friend

Central Truth
Since the Holy Spirit is a divine person, He can be known and experienced.

Lesson Outline
- The Holy Spirit is God
- The Holy Spirit is a Person
- Names of the Holy Spirit

Introduction
Unless a man and his wife agree, there will be strife in the home (see Amos 3:3). The same is true of our walk with the Spirit of God. Before we can live in close fellowship with the Spirit, we must first be in agreement with Him. And, before we can be in agreement with the Spirit, we must first come to know Him personally. The Holy Spirit wants to be more to us than just a "doctrine we believe" or a "tool we use." He wants to be our personal Friend and Guide. In this lesson we will begin our wonderful journey of knowing and experiencing the Spirit. We will do this by getting better acquainted with our Remarkable Friend—the Holy Spirit. In doing this we will answer the important question, "Who is the Holy Spirit?"

THE HOLY SPIRIT IS GOD

Some think of the Holy Spirit as some mysterious power, such as gravity, electricity—or even witchcraft. The Holy Spirit, however, is not such an impersonal force. He is, in fact, God. One writer described the Holy Spirit as "God in action."

The Third Person of the Trinity
The Holy Spirit is sometimes called the "third person of the Trinity." The Bible teaches that, although God is one in His divine essence (Deut. 6:4), He is three in person. He is God the Father, God

the Son, and God the Holy Spirit (Matt. 28:19; 2 Cor. 13:14).

So, just as the Heavenly Father is God, and Jesus the Son is God, the Holy Spirit is also God. When we speak of the power of the Holy Spirit, we are in reality talking about the power of God. When we talk about the voice of the Holy Spirit, we are talking about the voice of God. In fact, anytime we speak about the Holy Spirit we are speaking of God.

All the Characteristics of God

As God, the Holy Spirit possesses all of the divine attributes (or characteristics). For instance, as God, the Spirit is *eternal* (Heb. 9:14), that is, He has no beginning and no end—He has always been and He will always be. The Holy Spirit is *omnipresent.* This means that He is present everywhere at once. There is no place in all of the universe where the Holy Spirit is not (see Ps. 139:7- 8). Further, the Holy Spirit is *omnipotent.* As God, He has all power (Luke 1:37). Just think of it: when we are filled with the Holy Spirit, we are filled with all of the power of God. Anything that God asks us to do, we can accomplish with His help (1 John 4:4). Finally, as God, the Holy Spirit is *omniscient*, that is, all-knowing (1 Cor. 2:10). He is, therefore, never taken by surprise. As we walk in the Spirit, He will reveal to us the things we need to know to do the will of God.

THE HOLY SPIRIT IS A PERSON

A Divine Person

What do you think when you hear that the Holy Spirit is a person? Some people have no problem thinking of God the Father as a person, and they have no problem thinking of Jesus as a person, but they struggle in thinking of the Holy Spirit as a person. This could be because His name, the Holy Spirit, sounds more like a thing than a person. Paul, however, referred to the Holy Spirit as "the Spirit Himself" (Rom. 8:16, 26). Notice that Paul did not call the Holy Spirit, "the Spirit itself" (as the KJV wrongly translates) because He is not a thing, but a divine person. So, just as the Father and the Son are persons, the Holy Spirit is a person. It is, therefore, wrong to refer to Him as "it." We should always refer to the Spirit as "He" or "Him."

Personal Attributes

When we speak of the Holy Spirit as a person we do not mean that He is a human being with a physical body like you or me. We do mean, however, that, as a person, He has a mind and a personality. Here are some Scripture references which speak of the personal attributes and activities of the Holy Spirit:

- He has a mind (Rom. 8:27).
- He has a will (1 Cor. 12:11).
- He leads (Gal. 5:18).
- He teaches (John 14:26).
- He convicts (John 16:8).
- He guides (John 16: 13).
- He intercedes for believers (Rom. 8:26).
- He testifies (Rom. 8:16).
- He can be lied to (Acts 5:3).
- He can be resisted (Acts 7:51).
- He can be blasphemed (Matt. 12:31-32).

NAMES OF THE HOLY SPIRIT

We can learn much about our Remarkable Friend by studying the names He is given in Scripture. Just as Jesus has many names (such as Savior, Lamb of God, the Door, the Truth, and others), and each of these names reveals something about His character and work, so the Holy Spirit has many names, which also reveal something about His character and work. Let's look at seven:

1. The Spirit (John 3:5; 1 Cor. 2:10). When we use the name Spirit, we remember that He is not limited by a human body. He is at all places at all times.

2. Spirit of God (Gen. 1:2; Judg. 6:34; 1 Sam. 10:10, 16:13-14; Isa. 40:3; Ezek. 1:24; Matt. 3:6; Luke 4:18; Acts 8:39; 1 Cor. 2:14; Eph. 4:20). When we call Him the Spirit of God, we distinguish the Holy Spirit from all other spirits. He is the Spirit who proceeds from God, and is, in fact, God Himself.

3. Holy Spirit (Ps. 51:11; Isa. 63:10, 11; 1 Kings 11:13; Matt. 28:19; Rom. 1:4; Eph. 1:13; 4:30; and 1Thess. 4: 8). When we refer to Him as the Holy Spirit, we are reminded that He is absolutely without sin or evil of any kind. He is the one who imparts the holiness of God into the life of the believer (Rom. 8:13; 15:16).

4. Counselor (John 14:16,26; 15:26; 16:7). The word translated "Counselor"(NIV) literally means "one who walks along side another to help." As the Counselor, the Holy Spirit is the one who takes the place of Jesus. He will be everything to us that Jesus would be if He were here in person.

5. Spirit of Christ. (John 15:26; Rom. 8:9). As the Spirit of Christ, the Holy Spirit speaks about Christ, reveals Him to the unbeliever, and supplies the faith the repentant sinner needs to believe in Him. He then imparts the Christ-life to all who believe.

6. Holy Spirit of Promise (Eph. 1:13). The Holy Spirit was promised to God's people from ancient times (Joel 2:28-29). Jesus called the baptism in the Holy Spirit "the promise of the Father" (Luke 24:29; Acts 1:4).

7. Spirit of Truth (John 14:16, 17; 15, 26; 16:13). One of the Holy Spirit's works in believers is to live in them, to testify concerning Jesus, and to guide them into all truth.

In this lesson we have begun to get better acquainted with our Remarkable Friend, the Holy Spirit. We have learned that He is a divine person. And, because He is a person, He can be known and experienced. His desire is to work in our hearts and help us in every area of our lives. As we continue through this study, we will learn many new and exciting truths about life in the Spirit. Get ready to experience your new life in the Spirit!

Class Discussion

Discuss the following in class:
1. Why is it important that we understand that the Holy Spirit is God?
2. Why is it important that we understand that the Holy Spirit is a person?
3. How does knowing the various names of the Holy Spirit help us in relating to and experiencing Him?

Your Wonderful Life in the Spirit

Central Truth
Every believer should earnestly desire and ardently pursue a life in step with the Spirit.

Lesson Outline
- Life in the Spirit Defined
- The Blessings and Benefits of Life in the Spirit
- Prerequisites to Life in the Spirit

Introduction
When we purchase something in the market, we want to receive the maximum return on our investment. That's why we bargain for the lowest price possible! It is the same with God. He wants every person to receive the maximum return on his or her investment in life. This is one reason why Jesus came—to give us "life to the full" (John 10:10).

In this lesson we will learn more about the wonderful life that God offers to every believer, a life lived "in step with the Spirit" (Gal. 5:25). In doing this, we will answer three important questions: (1) What is meant by the term "in the Spirit?" (2) What are the benefits and blessings of a life lived in the Spirit? and (3) What must we do before we can live in the Spirit?

LIFE IN THE SPIRIT DEFINED

Sometimes we Pentecostals make statements such as this: "The pastor was really in the Spirit when he ministered today." Or we may accuse, "He was not in the Spirit when he did that!" And yet, when while make such statements, there is a problem. Many of us do not clearly understand the true meaning of the biblical phrase "in the Spirit."

The term, "in the Spirit" (or its companion term "by the Spirit") is used at least 29 times in the New Testament where the word "Spirit" refers to the Spirit of God. Sometimes when the Bible speaks of being in the Spirit, it simply means to be in a living relationship with Christ through the Spirit (Rom. 8:9; see also John 3:1-7; Rom. 2:29; Gal. 3:3; 1 John 3:24). In this sense all Christians are in the Spirit.

There is, however, a second meaning of the term. In this sense to be in the Spirit means to be under the influence, control, or guidance of the Holy Spirit. The phrase is used this way at least twenty times in the New Testament. This is the meaning that we will most often be using as we move through this study.

Thus, when we say that a person is in the Spirit, we could mean that he or she is under the influence or control of the Holy Spirit. For instance, Paul was once "compelled by the Spirit and testified to the Jews that Jesus is the Christ" (Acts 18:5). There are many other New Testament examples of people being influenced or controlled by the Spirit, for instance, Acts 20:22, 1 Corinthians 14:2, and Revelation 1:10, 4:1-2; 17:3; 21:10.

In other instances believers were in the Spirit and received guidance from Him. Jesus is the best example. Throughout His ministry He was guided by the Spirit. On one occasion, immediately after His baptism, Jesus was "filled with the Spirit" and then "led by the Spirit" into the wilderness (Luke 4:1). Other examples of believers being in the Spirit and receiving guidance from the Spirit include Luke 2:25-27, Acts 16:6-10, and Romans 8:14.

THE BLESSINGS AND BENEFITS
OF LIFE IN THE SPIRIT

Great blessings come into the lives of Christians who enter into the Spirit-filled life. Blessings also come to the church as more and more Christians learn to walk and live their lives under the Spirit's direction. Here are some benefits that come as a result of living one's life in the Spirit:

1. Power to witness (Acts 1:8)
2. God's abiding presence (John 14:16-18; 2 Cor. 13:14)
3. Divine guidance (Acts 9:11; 16:6-10)
4. Overflowing joy ((Rom. 14:17; 1Thess. 1:16; Acts 2:46)
5. Power over Satan (Luke 10:19; Matt. 12:28; 1 John 4:4)

6. A life of blessing to others (John 7:37- 38)
7. Power over temptation ((Rom. 8:1-4; Gal. 5:16)
8. True worship (John 4:24; Luke 19:21; Rom. 8:15)
9. Spiritual gifts (1 Cor. 12:7-10)
10. Spiritual fruit (Gal. 5:22-23; John15:4-5; cf. 14:17, 20)
11. Physical strength and healing (Rom. 8:11)
12. Prayer life strengthened (Luke 11:1-13; Rom. 8:26-28)
13. Spiritual man renewed (Eph. 3:16; 1 Cor. 14:4; Jude 20-21 with Rom. 5:5).

PREREQUISITES TO LIFE IN THE SPIRIT

With so many attendant benefits accruing , how could anyone not want to live in step with the Holy Spirit? There are, however, certain things one must do in order to enter into the Spirit-filled life. Let's look at five:

Born of the Spirit
Before one can enter into the Spirit-filled life he or she must first be born of the Spirit. Jesus said, "Flesh gives birth to flesh, but the Spirit gives birth to spirit" (John 3:7). We are born again when we come to God, repent of our sins, and put our trust in Christ alone for salvation. As a result, we become new creations in Christ (2 Cor. 5:17). We are made alive to God and to the things of the Spirit of God (Rom. 6:11-13; John 3:3).

Filled with the Spirit
In addition to being born of the Spirit, one must be filled with Spirit if he or she is going to live a life in step with the Spirit. With this powerful spiritual experience comes the power needed to be Christ's witness (Acts 1:8). In addition to being initially baptized in the Holy Spirit, the believer who desires to live in step with the Spirit, must learn to stay full of the Spirit (Eph. 5:18).

Openness to the Spirit
A third prerequisite to a life in the Spirit is genuine openness to the things of the Spirit. The person who has a closed mind or critical spirit will never be able to live a life in step with the Spirit of God (Heb. 3:8; 4:7).

Hunger and Thirst after God

As we hunger and thirst after God, we open ourselves to the Spirit and to His working in our lives (Matt. 5:6). Just as thirst for water draws the deer to a river, thirst for God will draw us to Him (Ps. 42:1). As a result, our lives become streams of spiritual water flowing out to those around us (John 7:37-39).

Ardent Pursuit of the Spirit

Before the Day of Pentecost the disciples were "continually in the temple praising and blessing God" (Luke. 24:53). After the Day of Pentecost, "every day they continued to meet together in the temple courts" (Acts 2:46). They were ardently pursuing the things of the Spirit. It must be the same with us today. We who would live a life in step with the Spirit must ourselves ardently pursue the things of the Spirit of God.

In this lesson we have learned that it is the privilege and responsibility of every believer to live and walk in step with the Spirit of God. Such a life is filled with great joy and blessing. In later lessons we will expand on some of the themes we have introduced here.

Class Discussion

Discuss the following in class:
1. Discuss why many Christians fail to live in step with the Spirit of God.
2. Discuss several benefits that come to the church and into a Christian's life from living in the Spirit.
3. Why is spiritual experience so necessary before one can live in step with the Spirit?
4. How does one's openness to the things of God influence his or her walk with the Spirit?

The Gateway to Life in the Spirit

Central Truth
Every believer should enter into the Spirit-filled life by being baptized in the Holy Spirit.

Lesson Outline
- What is the Baptism in the Holy Spirit?
- Why Is the Baptism in the Holy Spirit So Important?

Introduction
Just before Jesus returned to heaven He commanded His disciples to be baptized in the Holy Spirit (Acts 1:4-5). In this lesson we will discuss this powerful spiritual experience. We will learn that it is the gateway into the Spirit-filled life. In doing this we will answer two questions about this essential experience: (1) What is the baptism in the Holy Spirit? and (2) Why is the baptism in the Holy Spirit so important to a life in the Spirit?

WHAT IS THE BAPTISM IN THE HOLY SPIRIT?

Scripturally, five things can be said about the baptism in the Holy Spirit:

A Biblical Experience
When we say that the baptism in the Holy Spirit is a biblical experience we mean two things:

1. It is in the Bible. The experience of Spirit baptism is not an invention of any modern religious movement. It is found in the pages of the Bible. John the Baptist, Jesus, and Peter all spoke of the experience (Matt. 3:11; Acts 1:4; 11.16). Jesus promised power to those who received it (Acts 1:8). The disciples were first baptized in the Spirit on the Day of Pentecost (Acts 2: 1-4).

2. It is a command. All believers are commanded to be filled with the Holy Spirit. Before Jesus returned to heaven He commanded His disciples, "Do not leave Jerusalem, but wait for the gift my Father promised" (v. 4). Paul commanded believers to "be filled with the Spirit" (Eph. 5:18). Are you a believer in Christ? Then you, too, have been commanded to be filled with the Holy Spirit.

A Separate Experience

The Holy Spirit is a separate experience from the new birth. On three different occasions in Acts the new birth and the baptism in the Holy Spirit are shown to be separate experiences:

1. The Revival in Samaria (Acts 8:4-17). The Bible says that Philip went to Samaria and preached Christ to them (v. 5). They believed and received the message (v. 6, 12), experienced great joy (v. 8), and were baptized in water (v. 12). And yet, it was not until Peter and John arrived some days later and laid hands on them that they received the Holy Spirit (vv. 16-17).

2. Saul of Tarsus (Acts 9:1-19). Saul of Tarsus (Paul), was converted on the Damascus road, and was later filled with the Spirit in the city of Damascus when Ananias prayed for him. We know that he was truly converted when he encountered Jesus on the road because he called Jesus "Lord" (v. 5; ref. 1 Cor. 12:3), he obeyed Jesus and submitted fully to Christ's will (vv. 6-9), and Ananias called him "Brother Saul" (vv. 17; Acts 22:13). Some days later, when Ananias laid hands on him, he received the Holy Spirit (vv. 17-18). There was thus a period of time between Saul's conversion and his receiving the Spirit.

3. The Ephesian Disciples (Acts 19:1-7). The twelve Ephesian disciples were likely members of the emerging church in Ephesus (Acts 18:27). They had believed the message of John the Baptist concerning the Lord Jesus and had put their faith in Him. Paul, therefore, baptized them in water (vv. 4-5). It was after all of this that "the Holy Spirit came on them, and they spoke in tongues and prophesied" (v 6). Like the Samaritans and Saul before them, the Ephesians' experience of Spirit baptism was subsequent to and separate from their new birth.

A Normative Experience

When we say that the baptism in the Holy Spirit is a normative experience we mean that it is for all believers. Throughout the Bible the word "all" is often used in relation to receiving the Spirit (see Num. 11:29; Joel 2:28-29; Acts 2:4, 17; 10:44-47). Jesus said that the heavenly Father would give the Spirit to any of His children who would simply ask for it (Luke 11:9-13).

A Powerful Experience

Jesus said that the Holy Spirit would come upon the believer as "power from on high" (Luke 24:49). When one is filled with the Spirit, he or she is consumed with and overcome by God's mighty power and presence. The experience dramatically changed Peter and the others who were filled with the Spirit in the book of Acts. Once you have been truly baptized in the Holy Spirit, you will never be the same.

A Necessary Experience

It is essential that every Christian be baptized in the Holy Spirit (Luke 24:49; Acts 1:4-5). The baptism in the Holy Spirit is the believer's source of spiritual strength and the gateway into the Spirit-filled life.

WHY IS THE BAPTISM IN THE HOLY SPIRIT SO IMPORTANT?

Someone may ask, "Why this emphasis on the baptism in the Holy Spirit? Why should I be filled? What are the benefits I can expect in my own personal life from being filled with the Spirit?" The baptism in the Holy Spirit brings the following benefits into the life of the one who receives:

Greater Effectiveness

Being filled with the Spirit opens the way for greater effectiveness in our work for the Lord. The experience will empower the believer for effective service in three primary areas:

1. Power to witness. Jesus promised, "You will receive power when the Holy Spirit comes on you; and you will be my witnesses" (Acts 1:8). Every believer needs to be filled with the Spirit because every believer has been called to be Christ's witness (Luke 24:48; Acts 2:32; 5:32).

2. Power in prayer. When the disciples asked Jesus to teach them how to pray, He went on to teach them how to be filled with the Holy

Spirit (Luke 11:1-13). Paul taught that the Holy Spirit will help us in prayer (Rom. 8:26-27).

3. Manifestation of spiritual gifts. Spiritual gifts are given to Spirit-filled Christians to enable them to effectively accomplish the will of God (1 Cor. 12:7-10). Since the gifts of the Spirit are resident in the Spirit, and the Spirit is powerfully resident in those who have received Him, anyone who is filled with the Spirit can expect to be used by God in manifesting spiritual gifts.

Other Spiritual Benefits

The baptism in the Holy Spirit will also enable the believer to live a life more sensitive to the things of God (Matt. 9:36; John 16: 8; 1 Cor. 2:12). With the infilling of the Spirit comes a greater potential for spiritual understanding (John 3:8; 16:13; 1 Cor. 2:14), a deeper love for God (Rom. 5:5), and a greater consecration to His work (Acts 4:20; 5:29).

If being filled with the Holy Spirit will bring such blessings into the life of the Christian, who would not want to be filled? Have you been filled with the Spirit? If not, you can be today. A wonderful life in the Spirit is yours for the asking!

Class Discussion

Discuss the following in class:
1. Why do we say that the baptism in the Holy Spirit is a biblical experience?
2. Why is it necessary for every believer to be baptized in the Holy Spirit soon after conversion?
3. Discuss several benefits of being baptized in the Holy Spirit.
4. How is the baptism in the Holy Spirit the "gateway into the Spirit-filled life"?

How You Can Be Filled with the Holy Spirit Today

Central Truth
We can each receive the Holy Spirit today by acting in bold faith.

Lesson Outline
- Elements Involved in Receiving the Spirit
- When You Come To Be Filled with the Spirit
- Be Filled with the Spirit Today!

Introduction
The experience of the 120 on the Day of Pentecost set the pattern for all of God's people until Jesus comes again (Acts 2:1-4; 39). In this lesson we will talk about how you, and the ones to whom you minister, can receive this gift of the Holy Spirit believers. As you study this lesson, open your heart to God. Allow the Holy Spirit to fill and empower you, just as He did those first disciples on the Day of Pentecost.

ELEMENTS INVOLVED IN RECEIVING THE SPIRIT

It is helpful for someone wanting to be filled with the Spirit to know what is involved in receiving the Spirit. Scripturally, there are five essential elements involved in one's receiving the Holy Spirit:

Desiring the Spirit
Before one can be filled with the Spirit, he or she must desire the Spirit. They must sincerely desire a closer walk with God, and want to be more useful in His kingdom. Jesus said, "Seek and you will find; knock and the door will be opened unto you" (Luke 11:9, note v. 13). Seeking and knocking imply strong desire. Being filled with the Spirit begins on the inside, with a heart that is hungry for more of God (see Matt. 5:6; John 7:37).

Asking for the Spirit
Speaking of the Spirit, Jesus said, "Ask and it will be given to you...everyone who asks receives...your heavenly Father [will] give the Holy Spirit to those who ask Him!" (Luke 11:9-10, 13). God desires every one of His children to be filled with the Spirit. He is not withholding His blessing. He patiently waits for us to ask. Ask Him now! He will fill you with His Spirit today.

Exercising Faith
Jesus said that the experience is for the one "who believes" (John 7:38). Paul taught that the promise of the Spirit is received by "believing the message" (Gal. 3:2, 5, 14).

Receiving
Receiving the Holy Spirit is an act of bold faith. Jesus taught, "Whatever you ask for in prayer, believe that you have received it, and it will be yours" (Mark 11:24). God's hand is outstretched. He is waiting for you to take the gift from Him. Claim the fullness of the Spirit right now by the bold act of receiving.

Speaking
On the day of Pentecost "they were all filled with the Holy Spirit *and began to speak...*" (Acts 2:4). As they spoke, the Holy Spirit performed a miracle in their mouths. They "began to speak in other tongues as the Spirit enabled them." Once you have, by an act of faith, received the Holy Spirit, you will sense His presence deep inside. At that moment you should begin to boldly speak out, allowing the Spirit to take control and pray through you. You will begin speaking in a beautiful new language. The language will not come from your mind, but from deep inside your inner man (John 7:38; 1 Cor. 14:14).

WHEN YOU COME TO BE FILLED WITH THE SPIRIT

It is helpful to understand the following truths as you come to be filled with the Spirit:

If You Are Saved, You Are Ready
Anyone who has truly put his or her faith in Christ and repented of their sins is ready to be filled with the Spirit (Acts 2:38). There are no

other preconditions. If you have been truly born again, you are read right now to receive the Holy Spirit.

Being Filled Is Easy

We receive the Spirit by simply asking in faith (Luke 11:9-10). For the committed disciple being filled with the Spirit is not something abnormal or out of the ordinary. It is the natural thing for every Christian to do (John 20:22). Our heavenly Father is ready now to give His Spirit to those who ask (v. 13).

Leave Your Pride Behind

To be baptized in the Spirit one must leave all pride and vanity behind. Such things have no place in our walk with God, and they are the very things that hinder some from being filled with the Spirit (1 Pet. 5:5). Put your pride behind you, humble yourself before God, and be filled with the Spirit today (James 4:10).

Expect to Speak in Tongues

When you are filled with the Spirit, you should expect to speak in tongues as an evidence of your being filled (Acts 2:4). This was the recurring scriptural evidence throughout the book of Acts (Acts 10:46; 19:6).

You Will Receive Power

While speaking in tongues is the first sign of being baptized in the Holy Spirit, it is not its purpose. The primary purpose of Spirit baptism is empowerment for witness (Acts 1:8). Once you have been filled with the Spirit you should immediately begin to tell others about Christ. The Spirit will give you the power and boldness you need (Acts 4:31).

BE FILLED WITH THE SPIRIT TODAY!

To receive the Holy Spirit boldly approach God's throne, knowing that Jesus has made the way clear (Heb. 10:19). As you do, remember His promise: "Everyone who asks receives" (Luke 11:10). Don't doubt; the promise is yours (Acts 2:39).

Now, confidently ask the Father for His wonderful gift (Luke 11:9-13). As you pray, be aware of the Spirit's coming. You will sense His presence on you and in you. It is now time to reach out in faith and claim the promise as yours. Pray and believe this prayer, "I am now full of the Holy Spirit" (Mark 11:24). "Breathe" Him in (John 20:22). Sense His presence filling you (Acts 2:4).

Now begin to speak, allowing the Holy Spirit to "gush forth" from deep inside—from your innermost being (John 7:37, NASB). Allow the Spirit to speak through you, using your vocal organs and lips. When you begin speaking words in a language you have never learned, don't be afraid. God is filling you with His Spirit. Yield yourself more and more to Him and let the words flow out of you. Do it with all of your heart, holding nothing back, trusting God to do his part. Praise the Lord! You have been baptized in the Holy Spirit! You have tasted and discovered that the Lord is indeed good. Now go out and tell someone what God has done for you!

The baptism in the Holy Spirit is the gateway into the Spirit-filled life. It should thus be the aim of every Christian to be filled with the Spirit. And it should be the goal of every Christian leader to see that every believer has been baptized in the Holy Spirit.

Class Discussion

Discuss the following in class:
1. Discuss the five elements involved in being filled with the Spirit. Why is each element important?
2. How do you respond to the author's statement that "being filled with the Holy Spirit is easy"?
3. Why is it important to know that empowerment for witness is the primary purpose of Spirit baptism?
4. What should we do about Christ's command to be baptized in the Holy Spirit (Acts 2:4-5)?

Maintaining the Spirit-filled Life

Central Truth
It is the believer's responsibility to maintain his or her own life in the Spirit.

Lesson Outline
* The Importance of Maintaining the Spirit-filled Life
* Guidelines for Maintaining the Spirit-filled Life

Introduction
Things fall apart. That's a saying that is often heard in Africa. And it's true. Anything in this life left unattended falls apart—it deteriorates. The same is true of our spiritual lives. Unless they are constantly maintained, they deteriorate (see 2 Tim. 1:6). In this lesson we will discuss how the Spirit-baptized believer can maintain his or her walk in the Spirit.

THE IMPORTANCE OF MAINTAINING THE SPIRIT-FILLED LIFE

Must Be Constantly Renewed
The importance of maintaining the Spirit-filled life cannot be overemphasized. Once a believer has been baptized in the Holy Spirit he or she would be very unwise to assume that there is nothing more to do to maintain their life in the Spirit. The baptism in the Spirit brings one into a relationship with the Spirit that must be continually renewed (Acts 4:31) and maintained (Eph. 5:18).

Each Believer's Personal Responsibility
Every believer is personally responsible for maintaining his or her own spiritual life. Although pastors and Christian friends can encourage and inspire, the final responsibility lies with the individual Christian (2 Cor. 13:5). Failure to do this will eventually result in backsliding and a loss of power and relationship with the Lord. Just as

a fire needs constant monitoring if it is to remain ablaze, our spiritual lives also need constant attention if they are to remain ablaze (2 Tim. 1:6).

GUIDELINES FOR MAINTAINING A SPIRIT-FILLED LIFE

What specific steps can one take to ensure that that he or she continues to walk in the Spirit? Let's look at eight:

Seek Fresh Refillings

If a Christian is to remain full of the Spirit, he or she must seek fresh infillings of the Spirit. Note the following:

- On the Day of Pentecost the disciples were initially baptized in the Holy Spirit (Acts 2:4); and yet, they were refilled with the Spirit again and again (Acts 4:8, 31).
- Paul was first baptized in the Holy Spirit in the city of Damascus (Acts 9:17-18). He was again filled with the Spirit on the island of Cyprus (Acts 13:9).
- In Acts 19:6 the twelve Ephesian disciples were baptized in the Spirit. Paul later wrote the Ephesians, urging them to "be filled with the Spirit" (Eph. 5:18).

Every believer needs to be baptized in the Spirit, but they also need constant refillings with the Spirit. Spirit-filled Christians must continually ask, seek, and knock if they are to continue and progress in their spiritual lives (Luke 11:9-10).

Pray Without Ceasing

A second strategy one can employ in maintaining his or her Spirit-filled life is to "pray without ceasing" (1 Thess. 5:17, KJV). Paul urged Christians to "pray in the Spirit on all occasions with all kinds of prayers and requests" (Eph. 6:18).

Our daily prayer times should include prayer in tongues. Paul wrote, "He who [prays] in a tongue edifies himself" (1 Cor. 14:4). That may be one reason he said, "I would like everyone of you to [pray] in tongues" (v. 5), and testified, "I thank God that I [pray] in tongues more than all of you" (v. 18). Through prayer in the Spirit we maintain a powerful spirit-to-Spirit communion with God.

Be Fervent in Worship

Heartfelt worship is a third way a Christian can maintain his or her life in the Spirit. It is through Spirit-directed worship that we are "raised...up with Christ and seated...with Him in the heavenly realms" (Eph. 2:6). Such worship results in "times of refreshing... from the Lord" (Acts 3:19). When opportunities present themselves, we must enter into spiritual worship with our whole heart (Ps. 100:4). As we worship in the Spirit, our spirits are renewed, our faith is built up, our soul is refreshed, and we are readied for spiritual battle (Eph. 5:18-20).

Meditate on the Word

Daily meditation on the Word of God is another essential element for maintaining a Spirit-filled life. Jesus said that His words were "spirit and...life" (John 6:36). The same is true for all the words of Scripture. As we read the Bible, meditate on its words, and obey its teachings our spiritual lives are renewed and strengthened (Ps. 119:92-93; Matt. 7:26).

Walk by Faith

Another strategy for maintaining our lives in the Spirit is to walk by faith. To walk by faith and to walk by the Spirit are parallel concepts. Paul connected the walk of faith and the walk of the Spirit: "For we through the Spirit, by faith, are waiting for the hope of righteousness" (Gal. 5:5 NASB).

Live a Yielded Life

A sixth method we may use to maintain the Spirit's touch on our lives is to live a yielded life. Living a yielded life involves being submitted to the Spirit and His will. It further involves an attitude of openness to the Spirit's promptings. We must, therefore, live in a state of constant state of readiness to obey the voice of the Holy Spirit.

Cultivate a Sensitive Spirit

Another necessary requirement for living a Spirit-filled life is spiritual sensitivity. Spiritual sensitivity is the ability to sense in one's spirit what the Spirit is saying and doing. Anyone who wants to truly follow the Spirit must be keen to hear His voice. Just as we tune our radios to the proper station to receive a clear signal, in like manner, we must learn to tune in our spirits to the voice of the Spirit (Heb. 3:8, 15; 4:7).

Walk in Obedience

Obedient, holy living is another requirement for maintaining the Spirit-filled life. The Holy Spirit can be grieved and our spiritual lives can be blighted by impure living. Paul listed certain sins that grieve the Spirit of God, including unwholesome talk, bitterness, rage, anger, brawling, slander, and malice (Eph. 4:29-31). Such unholy attitudes and actions will quench the Spirit's moving in our lives, grieving Him and causing Him to depart. On the other hand, as we obey the voice of the Spirit, His presence grows stronger and we learn to better follow Him (Heb. 5:14).

Life is the Spirit is not automatic; it must be constantly maintained. We maintain our spiritual lives by giving diligent attention to them and to the things of the Spirit. We must never be guilty of allowing the flame of God's Spirit to go out in our lives.

Class Discussion

Discuss the following in class:
1. List and discuss reasons why is it important that the Spirit-filled Christian strive to maintain the Spirit's touch on his or her life?
2. Who is to blame if a believer loses the Spirit's touch on his or her life? Give reasons for your answer.
3. The author suggested eight strategies for maintaining one's life in the Spirit. Can you think of others?
4. Discuss three strategies for maintaining the Spirit-filled life that you feel are especially important in your own walk in the Spirit at this time.

The Fellowship of
the Holy Spirit

Central Truth
Every believer should walk in daily fellowship with the Holy Spirit.

Lesson Outline
- What Is Meant by the Fellowship of the Holy Spirit
- Why We Need the Fellowship of the Holy Spirit
- How We Can Live in Daily Fellowship with the Holy Spirit

Introduction
We can know God the Father, and we can know Jesus the Son, but can we really know the Holy Spirit? The answer is a resounding "Yes!" We can know the Spirit, and we can know Him intimately. Paul concluded 2 Corinthians with a benediction: "May the grace of the Lord Jesus Christ, and the love of God, and the fellowship of the Holy Spirit be with you all" (13:14). Notice the phrase *fellowship of the Holy Spirit.* This fellowship of the Spirit is a wonderful privilege of every Spirit-filled Christian. In this lesson we will discuss how one may live in daily fellowship with the Spirit of God.

WHAT IS MEANT BY THE FELLOWSHIP
OF THE SPIRIT

Fellowship of the Holy Spirit is more than a single experience in the Christian life. It is rather a life of intimate, daily communion with God through the Holy Spirit. The Greek word translated *fellowship* (2 Cor. 13:14) speaks of deep, loving communion or the sharing of common experiences. The fellowship of the Holy Spirit brings one into a loving relationship with each member of the blessed Godhead—the Father, the Son, and the Holy Spirit.

Fellowship with the Father
It is through the Holy Spirit that God pours out His love into our

hearts (Rom. 5:5). As the Holy Spirit moves in the believer's spirit, he or she is able to more fully comprehend God's love, and is inspired to respond to that love (1 John 4:19).

Fellowship with the Son

Before Jesus went to the cross He told His disciples, "I will not leave you as orphans; I will come to you" (John 14:18). He comes to us in the person of the Holy Spirit. That same night Jesus told His disciples that, when the Spirit comes, "he will bring glory to me by taking from what is mine and making it known to you" (16:14). The Spirit thus brings into loving communion with the Son.

Fellowship with the Holy Spirit

When the Bible speaks of the fellowship of the Holy Spirit, it is most certainly referring to the blessed communion that each believer can have with the Spirit Himself. The remainder of this lesson will focus on this wonderful relationship.

WHY WE NEED THE FELLOWSHIP OF THE SPIRIT

We must each learn to live in close fellowship with the Holy Spirit for at least two reasons:

We Need His Loving Companionship

Before Jesus returned to heaven He promised His disciples, "I will come unto you" (John 14:18). He further promised, "I am with you always, to the very end of the age" (Matt. 28:20). Today, Jesus comes to us, and is with us, in the person of the Holy Spirit. As our "other Counselor" (John 14:16) the Spirit comes to live with us, just as Jesus lived with His disciples when He was here in the flesh.

We Need His Strong Assistance

Consider this: the Holy Spirit does not come just to be with us, He comes to help us in every area of our Christian lives. Many benefits come from this relationship. For instance, the Spirit will come to empower us to be Christ's witnesses (Acts 1:8). He will also assist us in our preaching and teaching. This assistance includes increased persuasive power and divine insight into the Scriptures and into the needs of the people. Further, the Spirit will assist us by giving us power over the enemy (Matt. 12:28; Luke 10:19). Gospel ministry involves challenging and defeating evil spirits (Mark 16:17). Here again, the Spirit will be with us to help us to defeat Satan (1 John 4:4; Matt. 12:28-29).

HOW WE CAN LIVE IN DAILY FELLOWSHIP WITH THE SPIRIT

To live in daily fellowship with the Holy Spirit it is helpful to understand three pertinent issues:

The Prerequisites

It stands to reason that, before one can *continue* in fellowship with the Spirit, he or she must first *begin* his or her life in the Spirit (Gal. 3:3). Life in the Spirit begins with two essential spiritual experiences:

1. Being born of the Spirit (John 3:3-7; 2 Cor. 5:17). The unsaved person cannot know or understand the Spirit of God (John 14:17; 1 Cor. 2:14). However, as a result of being born again, one can "see" and experience the things of the Spirit (John 3:3).

2. Being filled with the Spirit. (Acts 1:4-5; 2:1-4). Spirit baptism increases one's capacity for spiritual things. As a result of being filled with the Spirit, the believer is more keenly aware of the Spirit's indwelling presence. His or her life is more fully energized by the Spirit's abiding presence.

The Problem

And yet there is a problem with many whose lives have been touched by the Spirit of God. Non-Pentecostals often assume that once they have been born again, they have "gotten it all" and, as a result, never progress in their spiritual experience. Many Pentecostals make a similar mistake. They think that once they have been baptized in the Holy Spirit they have "arrived" and that there is nothing more for them to do. They wrongly view the experience of Spirit baptism as a finish line, when, in reality, it is a starting line in the Christian life. Spirit baptism should not be viewed as simply a goal to be achieved, or a trophy to be attained. It is rather a glorious entrance into greater service and fellowship with God.

The Plan

Once a person has been born again and filled with the Spirit, he or she must aim to live in daily fellowship with the Spirit. To do this they must have a plan for building a strong relationship with the Spirit of God. This plan should involve two essential elements:

1. Prayer in the Spirit. Prayer in tongues is a major form of prayer in the Spirit (compare Rom. 8:26 with 1 Cor. 14:2-4). When Spirit-filled believers thus pray, the Spirit of God comes upon them, prays through them, and their relationship with God is strengthened (1 Cor. 14:14). At such a times an intimate communion takes place between the believer and the Holy Spirit.

2. Prayer to the Spirit. Not only should we pray *in* the Spirit, we should also pray *to* the Spirit. As we spend time in communion with the Spirit we build a more intimate relationship with Him. By doing this we can know Him better and better each day.

What a wonderful privilege we have, the privilege of living in daily fellowship with the Spirit of God. How foolish we would be if we neglect this wonderful opportunity. We should each make it our goal to live in daily fellowship with our Remarkable Friend, the Holy Spirit.

Class Discussion

Discuss the following in class:
1. In what ways is fellowship with the Spirit different from being born again or even filled with the Spirit?
2. How does the Holy Spirit bring us into a loving relationship with the Father? With the Son? With Himself?
3. Why does every believer need to live in constant fellowship with the Holy Spirit?
4. What are the prerequisites to one's living in fellowship with the Spirit?
5. How can a believer live in fellowship with the Holy Spirit?

Walking in the Spirit

Central Truth
It is every believer's privilege and responsibility to walk in step with the Holy Spirit.

Lesson Outline
- The Importance of Walking in the Spirit
- What It Means to Walk in the Spirit
- Requirements for Walking in the Spirit

Introduction
Paul encouraged the Christians in Galatia to live their lives in step with the Holy Spirit (Gal. 5:25). Not only were they to begin their Christian lives in the Spirit, they were to continue to live each day of their lives in the Spirit. In this lesson we will discuss the importance, meaning, and means of walking in the Spirit.

THE IMPORTANCE OF WALKING IN THE SPIRIT

Too often we Pentecostals emphasize being filled in the Holy Spirit but neglect teaching on the subject of walking in the Spirit. This has caused the spiritual lives of many to be stunted. If we are to grow in Christ, and live effective Christian lives, we must learn to walk in the Spirit.

Paul Appeals to Our Sense of Reason
Note how in Galatians 5:25 the apostle appealed to the Galatian believers' sense of reason. His argument was as follows: Since we begin our Christian lives through the enablement of the Holy Spirit, it makes sense that we should continue our lives in Him in the same way. Note the two parts of this argument:

1. We live by the Spirit. Paul reminds the Galatians how they began their Christian walk—they began it in the Spirit. There is, in fact, no other way to begin the Christian life (see John 3:3, 5-7). Further, as we have emphasized in previous lessons, every believer should begin his or her Christian life by being immediately baptized in the Holy Spirit

(Gal. 3:2, 14; 5:25; ref. Acts 2:38-39; 9:17-18; 10:44-47).
   2. We must walk by the Spirit. Paul challenged the Galatians, "Are you so foolish? After beginning with the Spirit, are you now trying to attain your goal by human effort?" (3:3). Since the Galatians had begun their new lives in Christ through the powerful inner working of the Holy Spirit, they should let the Spirit continue His work in and through them.

Jesus, Our Great Example
   Jesus is the living illustration of the concepts we are discussing in this study. He is our great example in three ways:
   1. He was filled with the Spirit. At the Jordan River Jesus received two baptisms: He was baptized in water and He was baptized in the Holy Spirit (see Luke 3:21-22). From that moment on, Jesus was filled with, and anointed by, the Holy Spirit (Luke 4:1, 14, 18-19; John 1:32-33; Acts 10:38). Before He returned to heaven, He commanded His followers to be filled with the Holy Spirit just as He Himself had been (Luke 24:49; Acts 1:4-5).
   2. He received direction from the Spirit. Jesus testified that everything He did, He did under the guidance of His heavenly Father (John 5:19-20, 8:28, 12:49). This divine guidance came to Him through the Holy Spirit (Matt. 4:1; Mark 1:12, Luke 4:1). Just as Jesus receive guidance from the Father through the Spirit, so should we.
   3. He ministered by the Spirit's power. Although Jesus was the eternal Son of God, He chose not to minister in His own divine power (Phil. 2:7) but through the power of the Holy Spirit (Luke 4:18-19; Acts 10:38). (This can be clearly seen in the gospel of Luke by reviewing the following texts: 3:21-22; 4:1-2, 14, 18; 5:17; 6:19.) Jesus choose to minister this way because He wanted to be an example for us. He wanted to show us how we, too, can minister in the same power and with the same results (John 14:12-16).

WHAT IT MEANS TO WALK IN THE SPIRIT

   What does it mean to walk in the Spirit? A close examination of Paul's teachings on the subject in the books of Galatians and Romans reveals that walking by the Spirit means at least four things:

To Walk in Holiness
   Paul instructed the Galatians, "Live by the Spirit, and you will not

gratify the desires of the sinful nature" (Gal. 5:16; see also 5:24). As they were guided by the Holy Spirit, they would be lead into a life of Christlike holiness. It is the same today, as we live our lives under the rule of the Spirit, we will be compelled (John 16:8-11) and empowered to live holy lives (Rom. 8:1-4, 13; Gal. 5:22-23).

To Walk in Love
To walk in the Spirit is to walk in love (compare Gal. 5:22 with 5:25). It is through the Holy Spirit that we experience God's love (Rom. 5:5), and it is by the same Spirit that we are kept in His love (Jude 20-21).

To Walk in Submission to the Spirit
The person who is walking in the Spirit has submitted his or her will to the will of the Spirit (Rom. 8:5; Gal 5:25). Self-will is the enemy of the Spirit-filled life. Until we are willing to fully submit our wills totally to the will of God, we will never fully walk by the Spirit.

To Walk in Faith
A life in the Spirit is a life of faith. Jesus said that the living waters of the Spirit would flow out of "whoever believes" (John 7:38). The Galatians began their life in the Spirit by "believing what [they] heard." They had, by faith, received the "promise of the Spirit" (Gal 3:14). In addition, God had given them His Spirit and worked miracles among them because they had "believ[ed] what they had heard" (v. 5). Our lives in the Spirit are from start to finish lives of faith.

REQUIREMENTS FOR WALKING IN THE SPIRIT

There are three essential requirements for walking in the Spirit:

Be Born of the Spirit
As we have indicated above, the first essential requirement for walking in the Spirit is to be born of the Spirit. No one should ever be so foolish as to think that he or she can walk in the Spirit without first being born of the Spirit. Have you been born from above (John 3:3-7)? Have you become a new creation in Christ (2 Cor. 5:17)? You can receive new life in Christ today by repenting of your sins and by putting your faith in Jesus Christ as Lord and Savior.

Be Filled and Refilled with the Spirit

Further, anyone who desires to walk in the Spirit must be continually filled and refilled with the Holy Spirit. Paul exhorted the Ephesian Christians to "be filled with the Spirit"—or literally, "be repeatedly filled with the Spirit" (Eph. 5:18). We can receive repeated fillings of the Holy Spirit by continually asking for the Spirit and seeking the face of the Father (Luke 11:9-13).

Sow to the Spirit

Paul further taught that we walk in the Spirit by sowing to the Spirit (Gal. 6:8). One way we can sow to the Spirit is by focusing our thoughts on the things of God (Rom. 8:5-9). Another way is to do those things that please the Spirit of God. These things include faithful, witnessing, holy living, acts of love and kindness, and quick obedience to the Word of God.

It should be the aim of every Christian to live his or her life under the Spirit's control. "If we live by the Spirit, we should also walk by the Spirit."

Class Discussion

Discuss the following in class:
1. Why is it important that every Spirit-filled Christian learn how to walk in the Spirit?
2. How is Jesus our great example of one who truly lived and walked in the Spirit?
3. How can a believer know if he or she is truly living a life in step with the Spirit?
4. Describe how a Christian can sow to the Spirit?

Speaking in Tongues, What Good Is It?

Central Truth
Every believer should daily practice prayer in tongues.

Lesson Outline
- What is Speaking in Tongues?
- What Good is Speaking in Tongues?

Introduction
A distinctive characteristic of the Pentecostal church is the belief that speaking in tongues is a valid and necessary practice for Christians today. This lesson will address this important issue. In doing this, it will answer two questions: (1) What is speaking in tongues? and (2) What good is it?

WHAT IS SPEAKING IN TONGUES?

A clear biblical understanding of the nature and purposes of tongues will aid the believer in his or her spiritual walk. It will also help them to explain the practice to others.

Often Spoken About in the New Testament
Speaking in tongues was the common practice of early Christians. Tongues are spoken of in five places in the New Testament:

1. The Great Commission. In His Great Commission Jesus told His disciples that believers would speak in tongues (Mark 16:17).

2. The Day of Pentecost. When the Holy Spirit was poured out on the Day of Pentecost, "All of them were filled with the Holy Spirit and began to speak in other tongues as the Spirit enabled them" (Acts 2:4).

3. The Book of Acts. Three times in the book of Acts we find believers speaking in tongues (Acts 2:4; 10:46; 19:6).

4. 1 Corinthians. In 1 Corinthians 12-14 Paul taught concerning the gift of tongues (12:10, 28, 30; 13:1, 8; 14:5-6, 18, 21-23, 39).

5. *Romans 8.* Paul said that "the Spirit himself intercedes for us with groans that words cannot express" (v. 26). He is likely referring to the practice of praying in tongues (compare with 1 Cor. 14:14).

The Bible teaches that speaking in tongues will continue as a practice in the church until second coming of Jesus (Acts 2:39; 1 Cor. 13:8-10).

Speaking in Tongues Defined

Speaking in tongues can be defined in four ways:

1. *A spiritual experience.* Speaking in tongues occurs when the Holy Spirit moves freely upon the spirit of a yielded believer (1 Cor. 14:14). Under the Spirit's impulse the Spirit-filled believer speaks in a language he or she does not know (Acts 2:1-4).

2. *A supernatural experience.* Paul described speaking in tongues as a "manifestation of the Spirit" (1 Cor. 12:7). It is thus a supernatural experience coming from the Spirit of God.

3. *A real language.* The Bible describes speaking in tongues as actual language. It can be in any human language or dialect (Acts 2:8), or it can be a heavenly language (1 Cor. 13:1).

4. *A universal experience.* Speaking in tongues is an experience for all Christians (Mark 16:17; Acts 2:4; 1 Cor. 14:5).

WHAT GOOD IS SPEAKING IN TONGUES?

Tongues in Private Devotions

Speaking in tongues sometimes functions as a personal prayer language (1 Cor. 14:18-19). Such tongues has been called *devotional tongues.* The Bible speaks of five personal benefits of such prayer:

1. *Builds one up spiritually.* Paul said, "He who speaks in a tongue edifies himself" (1 Cor. 14:4). As the Spirit-filled believer prays in tongues, he or she receives spiritual strength and blessing.

2. *Helps keep one conscious of the presence of the Holy Spirit within.* As one prays in tongues, he or she is acutely aware of the Spirit's dynamic presence within. Such an awareness can be a source of great joy and confidence.

3. *Helps one learn to more fully trust God.* As the believer puts his complete trust in God, and yields himself to the Spirit, he learns to more fully trust in God and His grace.

4. *A perfect outlet for praise and worship.* Paul taught that the person who speaks in an unknown tongue is "praising God with [his

or her] spirit" and giving thanks to Him (1 Cor. 14:16).

   5. A scriptural sign of the baptism in the Holy Spirit. The truly Spirit-baptized believer need never doubt whether he or she has been filled with the Holy Spirit. They will speak in tongues as the Spirit enables (Acts 2:4; 10:46).

Tongues in Public Worship

   Tongues can also properly function in as a gift of the Holy Spirit in public worship (1 Cor. 12:10, 28). Paul instructed the church concerning the proper use of the gift (1 Cor. 12-14). Its primary purpose in this context is the strengthening of the church (vv. 12, 26). It is to be used along with the gift of the interpretation of tongues (1 Cor. 14:5, 27). When properly exercised, the gifts of tongues and the interpretation of tongues bring three wonderful benefits to a congregation:

   1. Communicating divine truth. The tandem use of the gifts of tongues and the interpretation of tongues is a God-ordained method of communicating divine truth to a congregation. Through these gifts, God can communicate a prophetic word to a group of believers (1 Cor. 14:5, compare 1 Cor. 14:8, 21; Isa. 28:11-12).

   2. Prophetic prayer. Tongues with interpretation can also serve as a means of Spirit-directed prayer *for* a congregation. Paul notes that a person who speaks in tongues "does not speak to men but to God" (14:2). This use of the gift of tongues, sometimes called *prophetic prayer,* functions much like a message in tongues. It is, however, not a message to the church, but a Spirit-directed prayer to God in a language given by the Spirit. Like a message in tongues, it is interpreted into the language of the congregation. Great blessing comes to a congregation as believers realizes that the Spirit Himself praying for them through the gifts of tongues and interpretation.

   3. A sign that God is present. Tongues can also serve as a sign that God is present in the midst of His people and ready to speak (1 Cor. 14:22). Just as in ancient times a trumpet call signaled the fact that an important announcement was about to take place, tongues can be a signal to the unlearned that something important and supernatural is taking place. As a result, they are prepared to listen closely to the interpretation that follows. Further, when the speaker in tongues speaks in a language unknown to himself but known to an unbeliever, as on the Day of Pentecost, unbelievers hearts are opened to the gospel (Acts 2:11-12).

Prayer in tongues, whether used in private devotions or in public worship, can be a tremendous spiritual blessing. We should not neglect the use of this wonderful gift from God. In our private devotions we should pray in the Spirit daily. In our church services we should welcome the proper use of the gift of tongues with interpretation.

Class Discussion

Discuss the following in class:

1. Why is it important for believers to know the true nature and purpose of speaking in tongues?
2. Discuss the blessings that come to a believer who prays in tongues during his or her personal devotional times.
3. Discuss the blessing that come to a congregation when the gifts of tongues and the interpretation of tongues are properly administered.
4. Discuss how the gifts of tongues and the interpretation of tongues can function as prophetic prayer in a congregation. Why do you think that this use of these gifts has been neglected in Pentecostal churches? What has been the result?

Overcoming Temptation through the Power of the Spirit

Central Truth
We can each triumph over temptation through the power of the Spirit.

Lesson Outline
• What the Bible Says about Temptation
• Triumphing over Temptation

Introduction
In this lesson we will discuss an issue with which we are all familiar—the issue of temptation. We will first talk about temptation in general. Then, we will discuss how the Holy Spirit can give us victory over temptation and sin.

WHAT THE BIBLE SAYS ABOUT TEMPTATION

If we are to win the battle over temptation, it is helpful for us to understand five biblical truths concerning the nature of temptation:

We Must All Cope with Temptation
James wrote that "every man is tempted..." (1:14, KJV). Being tempted, however, is not, in itself, sin. One sins only when he or she lingers and yields to the temptation.

Victory is Possible
We are not helpless puppets to Satan, nor or we slaves to our own fleshly lusts, but we can win the battle against temptation. God has promised to provide a way out of every temptation (1 Cor. 10:13). Further, through the power of the Spirit we can triumph over temptation (Gal. 5:16).

Sources of Temptation

To triumph over temptation it is helpful to understand the three sources of temptation:

1. Our own carnal nature. James wrote that "each one is tempted when, by his own evil desire, he is dragged away and enticed" (1:14; ref. Rom. 7:7-9).

2. The world. Temptation also comes from the world, that is, from the systems and values of unregenerate society, which are under the control of Satan (1 John 5:19).

3. Evil spirits. A third source of temptation is the devil and demons. The Bible calls Satan "the tempter" (Matt. 4:3; 1Thess. 3:5, compare Gen. 3:1-7; Rev. 20:2). Believers are enticed by evil spirits to turn from God and His mission (1 Thess. 3:5; 1 Pet. 5:8).

The Battleground

Believers need to understand two things about their battle with temptation:

1. It is a mental battle. The vast majority of spiritual warfare occurs in people's hearts and minds, rather than in some distant, cosmic realm, as is often taught (2 Cor. 10:3-5).

2. It is a spiritual battle. Paul taught that our struggle "is not against flesh and blood, but against…spiritual forces of evil" (Eph. 6:4). The battle must, therefore, be fought with spiritual weapons (2 Cor. 10:4).

The Battle is Winnable

No Christian can ever truthfully say that "this temptation is too strong for me to resist." Paul reminds us that "God is faithful; he will not let you be tempted beyond what you can bear" (1 Cor. 10:13, see also 1 John 4:4). Neither can the believer say, "There is no way out of this temptation but to yield to it," for the Bible says, "But when you are tempted, [God] will provide a way out so that you can stand up under it" (1 Cor. 10:13). The battle with temptation is always winnable—if we will learn to live in step with the Spirit.

TRIUMPHING OVER TEMPTATION

The Bible speaks of four strategies a Christian may employ to emerge victorious over temptation and sin:

Be Filled with the Spirit

First, to triumph over the world, the flesh, and the devil the believer must be filled with the Spirit (Rom. 8:13). It is only through the power of the Spirit that we can live in victory over temptation and sin (see Gal. 5:16; 24-5:25).

Avoid Temptation

Next, we must avoid those things which tempt us to sin. Jesus taught us to pray, "Lead us not into temptation…" (Matt. 6:13). Paul instructed believers to "make no provision for the flesh to fulfill its lusts" (Rom. 13:13-14, NKJV).

Clothe Yourself in Christ

Paul wrote, "Clothe yourselves with the Lord Jesus Christ, and do not think about how to gratify the desires of the sinful nature" (Rom. 13:14). To clothe oneself in Christ is "put on the full armor of God" (Eph 6:11, 13, compare Rom. 13:12). If we will do this, we will be able to "take [our] stand against the devil's schemes" (v. 11).

Learn the Strategy of Resisting and Yielding

A final means of overcoming temptation is the spiritual strategy of *resisting and yielding.* This strategy works like this: In order to sin, a Christian will always have to make two wrong moves: he will have to yield to the temptation, and he will have to resist the Holy Spirit. In order to overcome the temptation, he will have to do just the opposite: he will have to resist the temptation and yield to the Spirit. The combining of these two spiritual disciplines—resisting and yielding—constitute an powerful strategy one can employ to overcome any temptation. Let's look more closely at each part of this strategy:

1. Resisting. To overcome temptation, the Christian must resolutely resist the temptation (1 Pet. 5:9; see also, James 4:7), that is, he or she must make a conscious choice not to yield to the temptation. Such resisting is essential; however, it is not enough. In Romans 7 Paul describes the futility of trying to resist temptation in our own strength (7:18 25).

2. Yielding. The second essential part of this strategy for overcoming temptation is yielding to the Spirit. It is heartening to know that, whenever we are faced with temptation, the Holy Spirit is always there to convict, provoke, and empower us to do what is right.

To win over the temptation we must consciously yield ourselves to this entreating of the Spirit. It is sometimes helpful to pray in the Spirit. As we yield ourselves to the power of the Spirit, the power of the temptation is weakened.

As we do this, a powerful spiritual principle takes over—called "the law of the Spirit of life" (Rom. 8:2). As a result, we are set free from sin and its grip (see Rom. 8:1-9). This is yet another reason why it is so important that every Christian be filled with the Holy Spirit. If we will "walk in the Spirit [we] will not fulfill the lusts of the flesh" (Gal. 5:16). James recommended this strategy in his epistle: "Resist the devil, and he will flee from you. Draw near to God and He will draw near to you" (4:7-8).

The practice of yielding to the Spirit is best learned in a Spirit-filled worship service. As Christians obey the voice of the Spirit, they learn how to more fully respond to the Spirit. Then, as they go out of the church into the world, they are better prepared to yield to the Spirit when they is tempted to sin.

Class Discussion

Discuss the following in class:
1. Why is it important that every believer know that he or she can win the battle over temptation and sin?
2. How does being filled with the Spirit help to prepare the Christian to face temptation?
3. Why is it important that a believer employ both parts of the spiritual strategy of *resisting and yielding* when faced with temptation? Which is the most important part? Give reasons for your answers.

Intercessory Prayer
in the Spirit

Central Truth
Intercessory prayer in the Spirit is the wonderful privilege of every Spirit-filled believer.

Lesson Outline
• What is Meant by the Term "Prayer in the Spirit"
• How Intercessory Prayer in the Spirit Blesses the Intercessor
• How Intercessory Prayer in the Spirit Blesses Others

Introduction
In this lesson we will discuss several benefits of praying in the Spirit. In doing this we will discuss three related issues: (1) What is meant by the term "prayer in the Spirit," (2) How prayer in the Spirit blesses the intercessor, and (3) How such intercessory prayer in the Spirit blesses others.

WHAT IS MEANT BY THE TERM "PRAYER IN THE SPIRIT"

When the Bible speaks of prayer in the Spirit, it uses the term in one of two ways:

Any Prayer Prompted by the Spirit
Generally speaking, prayer in the Spirit is any prayer that is prompted and directed by the Spirit of God. This kind of prayer is prayer in the Spirit because it is initiated and directed by the Holy Spirit. Paul described such prayer: "the Spirit helps us…the Spirit himself intercedes for us" (Rom. 8:26).

Prayer in the Spirit is thus a "team effort" between a Spirit-filled intercessor and the Holy Spirit. The Holy Spirit directs and prompts the prayer; the intercessor yields and cooperates. Sometimes the intercessor is prompted by the Holy Spirit to pray for a certain need. As he prays, the Holy Spirit comes powerfully upon him to anoint and direct his prayers. At such times the intercessor prays in the Spirit. Sometimes he may pray in his own language, and sometimes he may pray in tongues. Either way, he is praying in the Spirit.

Prayer in Tongues
When the Bible speaks of prayer in the Spirit, it is, more specifically, speaking of prayer in tongues. Paul defined prayer in tongues as prayer in the Spirit: "For one who speaks in a tongue speaks not to men but to God; for no one understands him, but he utters mysteries in the Spirit" (1 Cor. 14:2, RSV). He wrote further, "For if I pray in a tongue, my spirit prays, but my mind is unfruitful. So what shall I do? I will pray with my spirit, but I will also pray with my mind..." (vv. 14-15). In Romans 8:26 Paul describes prayer that is beyond human ability, that is, Spirit-prompted utterance. He is likely referring to the same prayer he described in 1 Corinthians 14:2, 14.

<h2 style="text-align:center">HOW INTERCESSORY PRAYER IN THE
SPIRIT BLESSES THE INTERCESSOR</h2>

When praying in the Spirit the intercessor receives help from the Holy Spirit, and thus prays with great power and effectiveness. As a result, the intercessor's own spiritual life is strengthened in at least three ways:

Built Up Spiritually
Paul wrote, "He who speaks in a tongue edifies himself" (1 Cor. 14:4). Great spiritual strength and blessing come into the life of the Christian who prays in the Spirit. We, therefore, like Paul, must boldly affirm, "I will pray with my spirit" (1 Cor. 14:14). Jude encouraged believers, "But you, beloved, building yourselves up on your most holy faith, praying in the Holy Spirit, keep yourselves in the love of God..." (vv. 20-21, NKJV). Here Jude cites two specific ways one is edified by praying in the Spirit:

Faith Increased
When we pray in the Spirit, we "build [ourselves] up on [our] most holy faith." As the Spirit-filled Christian prays in the Spirit, something wonderful happens: God supernaturally imparts faith into his or her spirit. Additionally, as the intercessor prays in the Spirit, he or she

prays "in accordance with God's will" (Rom. 8:27). It is, therefore, inevitable that their prayers will be answered (1 John 5:14-15). And, as a result their faith is increased.

Kept in the Love of God

Another personal benefit that flows from intercessory prayer in the Spirit is that the one praying is kept in the love of God (Jude 20). Paul tells us that "God has poured out his love into our hearts by the Holy Spirit, whom he has given us" (Rom. 5:5). As Spirit-filled believers pray for others in the Spirit, they experience the love of God in a fresh and dynamic way. As they draw near to God, He draws near to them (James 4:8), and their consciousness of and love for God grows stronger.

HOW INTERCESSORY PRAYER IN THE SPIRIT BLESSES OTHERS

While the one who intercedes for others receives personal blessing, this is not the main purpose of intercessory prayer in the Spirit. Its main purpose is to bless others. The Spirit prays through us for the needs of others. In Romans 8:26-27 Paul tells us how this works:

We Struggle in Prayer

Paul confessed, "We do not know what we ought to pray for" (Rom. 8:26). How many urgent needs do we fail to pray for simply because we are unaware of them? Even when we do know what to pray for, we often do not know how to pray because we do not know God's will in the matter. And all too often, as discussed in Lesson 8, we pray with the wrong motives, or, even worse, we simply lack any motivation to pray at all for others. We truly need the Spirit's help in our prayer lives.

The Spirit Helps Us Pray

At such times the Holy Spirit will come to our aid and intercede for us. As we yield ourselves to the Spirit, He prays through us in words that He gives (v. 27). A closer look at Romans 8:26-27 reveals five powerful ways the Spirit helps us in prayer:

1. He *"makes intercession for us."* As we yield ourselves to the Holy Spirit, He comes to us, fills us with His power and presence, and

prays through us. It is no longer us directing our own prayers, it is the Holy Spirit praying through us.

2. He does this "with groans which words cannot express." He prays through us in words and phrases which He inspires, that is, in expressions of His own creation.

3. He "searches our hearts." As we pray in the Spirit, the Holy Spirit searches the motives of our hearts. As we yield to His sanctifying power, our hearts are cleansed (Ps. 51:10-12), and, as a result, we are placed in a position where God can answer our prayers (Isa. 59:1).

4. He "knows the mind of the Spirit." The Spirit of God knows perfectly the mind and will of God in any given matter (1 Cor. 2:11).

5. He "intercedes for the saints according to the will of God." As we allow the Holy Spirit to pray through us, we pray for the needs of others according to His perfect will. Such prayers have great spiritual power (1 John 5:14-15).

Intercessory prayer in the Spirit can be a great blessing in the life of every Christian. We must not neglect this marvelous privilege.

Class Discussion

Discuss the following in class:
1. Can you remember a time when God used you in intercessory prayer in the Spirit? Share your testimony with the class.
2. Discuss reasons why many Spirit-filled Christians do not practice intercessory prayer in the Spirit. What can be done to remedy this situation?
3. What benefits can come into the life of the Christian and the church which regularly practices intercessory prayer in the Spirit?

Worship in the Spirit

Central Truth
    The Holy Spirit is the One who inspires and guides true worship.

Lesson Outline
*   The Essence of True Worship
*   The Spirit Inspires Our Worship
*   The Spirit Directs Our Worship

Introduction
    The Westminister Catechism reads, "Man's chief end is to glorify God, and to enjoy him forever." If this is true, then it must also be true that worship must be done properly. This lesson will discuss how the Holy Spirit helps us to properly worship God.

THE ESSENCE OF TRUE WORSHIP

God Must Be Worshiped in Spirit
    The only proper way to worship God is to worship Him in the Spirit. In John 4:23-24 Jesus gave to the world His greatest revelation concerning the nature of true worship. There He revealed four powerful truths concerning worship:
    1. God is spirit. He is, therefore, not limited by a physical form. Nor is He bound to a single locale or time frame. He can be worshiped in any place at anytime.
    2. God is seeking true worshipers. God is looking for people who will worship Him, not by outward form, but by inner devotion and sincerity.
    3. True worship must be done in Spirit and in truth. Since God is spiritual, those who worship Him must worship Him in Spirit. Since He is absolute truth, they must worship Him in truth.
    4. It is now time for such worship. The time to worship God in Spirit and in truth is now.

The Meaning of the Term "Worship in the Spirit"

Jesus said that God must be worshiped "in s[S]pirit." This phrase can mean either worship flowing from the human spirit or worship directed by the Holy Spirit. A careful examination of Scripture indicates that both concepts are true, as follows:

1. Worship from our human spirits. To worship in spirit (with a lowercase "s") means that we worship God out of our hearts, in total sincerity and honesty. True worship involves our human spirits reaching out in love and faith to God, who is Himself spirit. True worship is not based on dead ritual but on a living relationship between a person and God.

2. Worship by His Holy Spirit. Worship in Spirit (with an uppercase "S") indicates that true worship is prompted and energized by the Spirit of God. Paul reminded the Philippian believers that we "worship by the Spirit of God" (Phil. 3:3), that is, the Spirit of God initiates, inspires, and directs our worship. Mary and Zacharias were prompted by the Holy Spirit to praise God (Luke 1:46-55; 67-79). Jesus Himself was filled with joy and "through the Holy Spirit" began to praise His Heavenly Father (Luke 10:21). God cannot be truly worshiped without help from the Holy Spirit.

THE SPIRIT INSPIRES OUR WORSHIP

How the Holy Spirit Inspires Our Worship

The Holy Spirit inspires our worship in three ways:

1. The Spirit brings us into a loving relationship with God. Paul wrote of the "Spirit of adoption" who leads us into an intimate relationship with God (Rom. 8:15). As the Spirit of God moves in our hearts, we are made to feel the love of God (5:5) which causes us to cry out, "Abba, Father" (8:15).

2. The Spirit lifts up Jesus. The Spirit brings glory to Jesus (John 16:14). He does this by revealing to us His greatness, causing us to cry out, "Jesus is Lord!" (1 Cor. 12:3). Jesus is exalted in our hearts, and our mouths are filled with praise to Him.

3. The Spirit prompts us to worship. Throughout the Bible the Holy Spirit inspired people to worship. He inspired Miriam to lead the women of Israel in worship (Exod. 15:20). He came powerfully on upon King Saul, causing him to join in worship with a band of prophets (1 Sam. 10:5-11). On the Day of Pentecost those who were filled with the Spirit began "declaring the wonders of God" in the languages of the surrounding Gentile nations (Acts 2:11). The Spirit also inspired the churches in Corinth and Philippi to worship God (1 Cor. 14:16, 17; 25-26; Phil. 3:3). The same is true today. Those who have learned to yield themselves to the Spirit of the Lord have discovered a glorious freedom in expressing their worship to God (2 Cor. 3:17).

The Importance of Personal Preparation

We must prepare our hearts to worship God in Spirit and in truth (1 Cor. 14:26). This personal preparation should include prayer, meditation on the Word of God, and a fresh infilling with the Holy Spirit (Eph. 5:18-20).

THE SPIRIT DIRECTS OUR WORSHIP

The True Worship Leader

We begin our worship by acknowledging the Holy Spirit as the true Worship Leader. Everything we do must therefore be done in submission to Him and under His direction. In this context Paul instructed the Corinthian church concerning the operation of spiritual gifts. In their gatherings the Holy Spirit would distribute gifts to each one "just as he determines" (1 Cor. 12:7, 11). In other words, He would direct their worship. In the church at Antioch the Spirit directed one of their worship services (Acts 13:1-3). Note how the Spirit set the tone for the service and gave directions on how to proceed. The same order should mark our worship services today. If we are to truly worship in the Spirit, we should look to the Spirit of God as our Worship Leader.

Following the Leader

Since the Holy Spirit is the true Worship Leader, it is essential that the human worship leader be able to follow His directions. The worship leader must be very sensitive to the Spirit and must never wrest the service out of His hands. It is also necessary that the congregation be taught how to follow and respond to the promptings of the Spirit. In addition, if we want to ensure that the Spirit of the Lord is present in our worship services, and that we properly respond to His presence and follow His leadership, we must do the following:

1. We must appropriate the Spirit's presence. We appropriate the Spirit's presence in two ways: First, we pray. This prayer should take place before and during the worship service. Before the service we should spend time in prayer, preparing our hearts for the coming worship experience. As the service begins it is appropriate to lead the congregation in a prayer of invocation inviting the Holy Spirit to come and have His way. We can, as a result, legitimately expect the Spirit to come and manifest His presence in our midst (see Matt. 18:19-20).

Second, we can appropriate the Spirit's presence through praise and adoration (see Ps. 22:2, KJV). As Paul and Silas prayed and sang hymns to God in the Roman jail, the Holy Spirit powerfully manifested His presence (Acts 16: 26). We too, as we sing and shout our praises to God, can expect the Holy Spirit to come and manifest His presence in our midst.

2. We must respond to the Spirit's presence. Once the Spirit comes, we must properly respond to Him. We can do this in three practical ways: First, we can acknowledge the Spirit's presence. Just as we would never be guilty of ignoring a guest who came into our home, we should never be guilty of ignoring our Remarkable Friend when He comes into our worship services. Next, we should remember that He is sovereign, that He has a will for every church service, and that He comes to fulfill that will. Finally, we must be prepared to release spiritual gifts as the Spirit directs and prompts.

We must know that it is only with the help of the Spirit of God that we can truly worship God. We must, therefore, be ever desirous of His presence and open to His leadership in our worship.

Class Discussion

Discuss the following in class:
1. Why is it important that we understand the two meanings of worship in the Spirit as presented in the lesson?
2. With what attitudes must we come to church if we are going to really worship God in Spirit and in truth. What actions must we take?
3. What kind of person will make the best worship leader?

Ministry in the Spirit

Central Truth
We can minister effectively only as we are filled with the Spirit and learn to minister in the Spirit's power.

Lesson Outline
- The Holy Spirit Equips Us for Ministry
- The Holy Spirit Enables Us in Ministry
- How to Ensure the Spirit's Help in Ministry

Introduction
Someone has rightly observed that we can do the work of God in one of two ways: we can do it in our own strength, or we can do it in the Spirit's strength. In this lesson we will learn how we can appropriate the Spirit's strength in ministry.

THE HOLY SPIRIT EQUIPS US FOR MINISTRY

Power to Get the Job Done
Jesus concluded His earthly ministry with two commands: He first commanded His followers to preach the gospel to all nations (Matt. 28:18-20; Mark 16:16-18). He also commanded them to wait until they had been empowered by the Holy Spirit (Luke 24:49; Acts 1:4-8). Before they could fulfill Jesus' first command, they had to obey His second. The same is true for us today. Through Spirit baptism we are empowered to get the job done.

The Examples of Jesus and the New Testament Church
We can see more clearly how the Holy Spirit equips us for effective service by looking at the examples of Jesus and the New Testament believers.

The example of Jesus Jesus came to earth to give His life as a ransom for all people (Matt. 20:28, 1 Tim. 2:6). He also came to be an example to us as to how we should live and minister in the power of the Holy Spirit (John 13:15, 14:12, 16; Acts 10:38). Jesus was first anointed by the Spirit (Luke 3:21-22), He then went out and ministered in the Spirit's power (4:1, 14, 18-19; 5:17). In doing this,

He set the pattern of ministry for those of us who would follow Him (John 14:12).

The example of the New Testament church. Like Jesus, the early church ministered in the power of the Holy Spirit. The church was first empowered on the Day of Pentecost (Acts 2:4). They then went out and ministered with great power and effectiveness. They were simply following the pattern set by Jesus—first be empowered, then minister. We, too, have been called to minister in the power of the Holy Spirit, just as did Jesus and the early believers.

THE HOLY SPIRIT ENABLES US IN MINISTRY

Not only does the Holy Spirit give us the power we need to minister, He also enables us in the performance of our ministries. He does this in at least five ways:

He Inspires Us to Do Ministry
The Holy Spirit inspired Peter to go in faith to Caesarea and preach to the Gentiles there (Acts 11:12). Today, the Spirit will inspire us to do ministry. He does this by giving to us a burden for the lost, a love for the church, and a vision for the world.

He Empowers our Witness to the Lost
Jesus promised, "You will receive power when the Holy Spirit comes on you; and you will be my witnesses" (Acts 1:8). We can become powerful witnesses for Christ only if we will allow the Holy Spirit to fill us and use us in His harvest field. This empowering includes insight into the Scriptures (Acts 8:29-34, compare with Prov. 11:30; 1 Cor. 12:8), anointing to speak persuasively (Acts 6:10), and gifts of the Holy Spirit to supernaturally confirm the gospel that we preach (Acts 8:6).

He Anoints Our Preaching and Teaching
If we will prepare ourselves and yield to Him, the Holy Spirit will anoint our preaching and teaching in the same way He anointed the preaching and teaching ministries of Jesus (Luke 4:17-18; Acts 10:38) and the apostles (Acts 4:8, 31-33).

He Manifests Himself through Spiritual Gifts
The outpouring of the Spirit at Pentecost resulted in a dramatic release of miraculous power in the disciples' ministries. This release

of power manifested itself in speaking in tongues (Acts 2:4), anointed preaching (2:14ff, 4:31, 6:10, 8:25), powerful healings (3:1-8; 5:15; 6:7), signs and wonders (2:43, 5:12, 6:8, 8:6), exorcisms (5:16, 6:7), supernatural deliverance from danger (5:19), visions (6:55-56), and Holy Spirit baptisms (2:4, 8:17). Today, if we will be filled with the Spirit, and boldly proclaim Christ to the lost, we too can expect the same supernatural results.

HOW TO ENSURE THE SPIRIT'S HELP IN MINISTRY

We can prepare ourselves to receive the Spirit's help in ministry in three ways:

By Being Filled with the Spirit
The baptism in the Holy Spirit a basic requirement for any spiritual ministry (Acts 1:8; 2:4). No one should attempt to minister for Christ without this powerful enablement.

By Walking in the Spirit
Further, if we are to minister in the power of the Holy Spirit, we must learn to daily walk in the Spirit. Walking in the Spirit demands a life of holiness, prayer, yieldedness to the Spirit, and periodic refillings with the Spirit.

By Appropriating the Spirit's Help
The committed disciple who has been filled with the Spirit, and has learned to live in step with the Spirit, can expect ministry opportunities to come his or her way. At such times the Holy Spirit will direct the Christian worker on how to properly respond. He or she must appropriate the Spirit's help through acts of obedience and faith. These two elements—obedience and faith—are key to releasing the power of the Spirit into a ministry situation. Let's look briefly at how this works:

1. Obedience. When we act in obedience to the Word and the inner promptings of the Spirit, the Holy Spirit comes to anoint us for ministry. For example, as we obey Christ's command to witness for Him (Mark 16:15; Luke 24:48) the Spirit comes upon us to anoint and empower us to witness (Acts 1:8; 4:8). The opposite is also true. If we disobey, and refuse to witness, the anointing does not come. Many Spirit-filled Christians have failed to become effective witnesses for Christ simply because they have refused to obey His command to witness to those with whom they come into contact. If, however, they will obey His command, the Spirit will come to anoint and empower their witness. The principle is this: we must first obey, then the Spirit will come to enable us.

2. Faith. The anointing that comes through an act of obedience is released by an act of faith. Like an electrical switch, an act of faith on the part of the Christian worker releases into the situation the anointing to preach, prophesy, heal the sick, etc.

It works like this: A ministry opportunity presents itself. The Spirit-filled disciple discerns the Spirit's voice prompting him to minister. He now has a choice: he can obey the Spirit's voice, or he can ignore it. If he obeys, the anointing will come; if he disobeys, the anointing will subside. Once the Christian worker obeys the Spirit's voice and begins to minister, he must act in faith. Through a bold act of faith the anointing is released into the life of the needy individual and the need is met.

Jesus has commanded us to preach the gospel to the nations. He has instructed us to minister in the same power and anointing that He ministered. We can do this only through the enablement of the Holy Spirit.

Class Discussion

Discuss the following in class:
1. In what ways does the Spirit enable us to do spiritual ministry today?
2. Why have many Spirit-filled Christians failed to become powerful witnesses for Jesus as promised in Acts 1:8? Explain your answer.
3. What are the roles of obedience and faith in ministering in the power and anointing of the Holy Spirit?

Gifts and Fruit of the Spirit

Central Truth

Every believer should manifest spiritual gifts and display spiritual fruit in his or her life.

Lesson Outline

- Gifts and Fruit Defined
- Manifesting Gifts and Cultivating Fruit

Introduction

As the gifts and fruit of the Spirit are manifested in the lives of believers, the church is blessed and its witness to the world is enhanced. In this lesson we will discuss two issues concerning the gifts and fruit of the Spirit: how spiritual gifts and spiritual fruit relate to one another and how they operate in the Christian life.

GIFTS AND FRUIT DEFINED

Gifts of the Spirit

The nine gifts of the Spirit listed in 1 Corinthians 12 represent the various ways the Spirit of God manifests His presence in the midst of His people. They can be defined as supernatural anointings given by the Spirit of God through Spirit-filled believers to accomplish the will of God. (See 1 Cor. 12:7, 11; 14:26). They are manifested as believers respond in faith to the promptings of the Spirit. These gifts include the following: (1) *revelation gifts,* including a word of knowledge, a word of wisdom, and the distinguishing between spirits; (2) *power gifts,* including faith, gifts of healing, and miraculous powers; and (3) *prophetic gifts,* including prophecy, different kinds of tongues, and the interpretation of tongues. Every Spirit-filled believer should covet these gifts and anticipate being used by God to release them in ministry (1 Cor. 14:1, 39).

Fruit of the Spirit

Paul also speaks of nine fruit of the Spirit. These include love, joy, peace, patience, kindness, goodness, faithfulness, gentleness and self-control (Gal. 5:22-23). These Christlike qualities of character are produced in believers' lives as they abide in Christ (John 15:1-8) and live under the Spirit's direction (Gal. 5:16, 23).

MANIFESTING GIFTS AND CULTIVATING FRUIT

Both Are Needed

Both spiritual gifts and spiritual fruit are needed for two reasons: *1. A total witness of the gospel.* As we go into the world to preach the gospel, we must present a total witness of the gospel. This witness must include both a demonstration of Christ's power through the manifestation of spiritual gifts and a demonstration of Christ's character through the exhibition of the spiritual fruit. Only then will our hearers be able to understand the true nature of the Christian faith.

2. The full image of Christ. People were attracted to Jesus for three reasons: because of His gracious words (Luke 4:22; John 6:63; 7:46), because of His mighty works (Matt. 4:25; Mark 1:45), and because of His beautiful life (Mark 7:37; John 18:38, NKJV). If we are to present the full image of Christ to a dying world, we must do as Jesus did. Through the gifts of the Spirit we are able to speak His gracious words and demonstrate His powerful works. Through the fruit of the Spirit we are able to demonstrate His beautiful life.

Ministering Spiritual Gifts

Any believer who has been truly filled with the Spirit, and is walking in step with the Spirit, can be used by God in ministering spiritual gifts (1 Cor. 12:7). Since the gifts reside in the Spirit, and the Spirit resides in the believer, then all of the gifts reside in every Spirit-filled believer. They are released by the Spirit according to His sovereign will (1 Cor. 12:11), the believer's eager desire (1 Cor. 12:31; 14:1, 39), and as a result of the believer's responding in faith to the prompting of the Holy Spirit.

At times the Spirit will come as an anointing on the yielded believer. Once the anointing is sensed the believer must act in obedience and faith to release the spiritual gift. The act of faith could be to say or do a particular thing. It could even be a humanly impossible act. The believer must, nevertheless, act in boldness and faith. Once he or she acts, the anointing is released, the spiritual gift is manifested, and the work is accomplished.

Cultivating Spiritual Fruit

Spiritual fruit can only be cultivated by spiritual means. As one is born of the Spirit and filled with the Spirit, the seeds of the Spirit are planted in his or her life. The soil must then be cultivated in order for these seeds to grow and produce a harvest. Spiritual fruit may be cultivated in three ways:

1. By walking in the Spirit. As we walk in the Spirit and live our lives under the Spirit's control (Gal. 5:16-18) spiritual fruit are produced and mature in our lives (vv. 22-23). Walking in the Spirit involves crucifying the flesh with its passions and desires (v. 24), setting one's mind on what the Spirit desires (Rom. 8:5), being controlled by the Spirit (v. 8), putting to death the works of the flesh (v. 13), and being led by the Spirit (v. 14).

2. By abiding in Christ. A second way one can cultivate spiritual fruit in his or her life is by abiding in Christ. Jesus taught that, as we abide in Him, spiritual fruit is produced in our lives (John 15:1-8).

3. By attending to the means of grace. Means of grace are those spiritual disciplines which cause us to mature and grow in grace. They include the following:

- *Prayer and worship.* We should spend much time in private and corporate prayer and worship. Through these spiritual disciplines we provide the proper spiritual climate for spiritual fruit to grow in our lives.
- *Fellowship with other believers.* "As iron sharpens iron, so one man sharpens another" (Pr. 27:17). As brothers and sisters in Christ spend time together, they sharpen one another through godly example and council, and they encourage one another in the Christian life. As a result, spiritual fruit is fostered and cultivated in their lives.
- *Bible reading and meditation.* As a disciple reads and meditates on Scripture, his or her life is transformed and strengthened.

Both spiritual gifts and spiritual fruit are necessary qualities of the Christian life. If we as Christ's body are to fully represent Him to the world, we must possess both in abundance. As unbelievers see spiritual gifts in operation, they are brought face to face with Christ's awesome power. As they see the fruit manifest in Christians, they are made to see His beautiful character. If the world is ever to truly see

Christ in His church, we must earnestly covet both spiritual gifts and spiritual fruit in our lives.

Class Discussion

Discuss the following in class:

1. Compare and contrast spiritual gifts and spiritual gifts as to their origin and purpose in the believer's life.
2. Why is it important that both spiritual gifts and spiritual fruit be manifested in the lives of Christians?
3. What is the role of the Spirit in manifesting spiritual gifts? The role of the Spirit-filled believer? The role of obedience? The role of faith?
4. What must a believer do to cultivate spiritual fruit in his or her life?

– Other Books by the Denzil R. Miller –

Teaching in the Spirit (2000)

Power Ministry: How to Minister in the Spirit's Power (2004)
(available in English, French, Portuguese, Swahili, Malagasy,
Kinirwanda, and Chichewa)

*Empowered for Global Mission: A Missionary Look at the
Book of Acts* (2005)

From Azusa to Africa to the Nations (2005)
(available in English, French, Spanish, and Portuguese)

Acts: The Spirit of God in Mission (2007)

In Step with the Spirit: Studies in the Spirit-filled Walk (2008)

*The Kingdom and the Power: The Kingdom of God: A
Pentecostal Interpretation* (2009)

*Power Encounter: Ministering in the Power and Anointing
of the Holy Spirit: Revised* (2009)

*You Can Minister in the Spirit's Power: A Guide for
Spirit-filled Disciples* (2009)

The 1:8 Promise of Jesus: The Key to World Harvest (2012)

All of the above books are available from the
PneumaLife Publications
3766 N Delaware Avenue
Springfield, MO, 65803, USA

www.ingramcontent.com/pod-product-compliance
Lightning Source LLC
Chambersburg PA
CBHW060724030426